AN ATLAS OF MANKIND

Volume Three

MODERN EUROPE

AN ATLAS OF MANKIND

Volume Three

MODERN EUROPE

R. PETERSON

THE CLIVEDEN PRESS

AN ATLAS OF MANKIND

ISSN 0893-4649

Volume Three

MODERN EUROPE

R. Peterson

Copyright © 1987 by The Cliveden Press

1133 13th Street, N.W., C-2
Washington, D.C. 20005

Vol. 1   The Face of Africa (ISBN 0-941694-04-6
Vol. 2   The Classical World (ISBN 0-941694-15-1
Vol. 3   Modern Europe (ISBN 0-941694-31-3

Forthcoming

Vol. 4   The Asian Mainland
Vol. 5   Southeast Asia, Oceania and Australasia
Vol. 6   The Americas

ISBN 0-941694-31-3

Manufactured in the United States of America

ILLUSTRATIONS

ENGLAND
1. Anglo-Saxon male
2. Rupert Brook
3. Yorkshireman
4. A group of English children

SCOTLAND
5. Scotsman from Ayrshire
6. Officer of the Argyle and Sutherland Highland Regiment

WALES
7. Young male from Merionethshire

IRELAND
8. Anglo-Irish officer
9. Old lady from County Clare
10. Irish woman from County Kerry
11. Aran Islander

FAEROE ISLES
12. Faeroe Isles boy

ICELAND
13. Icelandic child

NORWAY
14. Odd Nansen
15. Norwegian woman from Bergen
16. Johan Hjort
17. Leif Larsen

SWEDEN
18. Swedish woman with classic Nordic features
19. Swedish male from Södermanland
20. King Gustav VI
21. Another Swedish female

DENMARK
22. Young Danish girl from rural district of Lyoe

GERMANY

23. Frisian male
24. "Borreby" male
25. Two German girls from Berlin
26. Faces in a German street
27. Prussian "Junkers" or officer-aristocrat
28. Silesian girl
29. Young Bavarian family
30. Elderly lady from the Allgau mountain region

AUSTRIA

31. Officer of the Austrian Army

THE NETHERLANDS

32. Young Dutch female

BELGIUM

33. Flemish poet

FINLAND

34. Kalevi Sorsa
35. Two young Finns, male and female

ESTONIA

36. Estonian peasant male

LATVIA

37. Two Latvian males

LITHUANIA

38. Group of Lithuanian women and girls

FRANCE

39. French aristocrat illustrating the "Frankish" type
40. French female of "Alpine" type
41. "Dinaric" type male from Central France
42. Breton pipers
43. Breton matron
44. French Basque male

SPAIN

45. Spanish Basques
46. Spanish female from Salamanca
47. Spanish female from Andalusia
48. Group of Balearic women

ILLUSTRATIONS   7

PORTUGAL
49. Two Portuguese fishermen
50. Rural Portuguese female of traditional type

SWITZERLAND
51. Swiss girl from the French-speaking Jura district
52. Young German-speaking male from Basle
53. German-speaking male from the Engadine
54. Italian Swiss females from Valois

ITALY
55. Woman from the Dolomites
56. German-speaking Tyrolean males
57. Piedmontese girl from Lanzo
58. North Italian male from Verona
59. Woman from the Tiber Valley
60. Female from Southern Italy
61. "Dinaric" male from Naples
62. Female from rural Calabria
63. Young Calabrian woman
64. Young Sardinian girl reflecting traditional Mediterranean genotype
65. Group of young Sardinian males

POLAND
66. Polish man and woman
67. Polish village children
68. Polish game warden
69. Two city males
70. Ruthenian man and woman

CZECHOSLOVAKIA
71. Young Czech girl
72. Moravian male
73. Two elderly Slovakian males
74. Bohemian husband and wife
75. A Vlach in national costume

HUNGARY
76. Hungarian male
77. Two Hungarian girls

ROMANIA
78. Young males from Bukovinia
79. Romanian male from Tulcea
80. A young village girl from Transylvania
81. Peasant elder from Transylvania

YUGOSLAVIA

82. Serbian Horsemen from Sinj
83. A group of Serbian men
84. Slovenian girl
85. Croat woman
86. Young Croat female
87. Male from Herzegovinia
88. Two Montenegrin males
89. Group of Macedonians

ALBANIA

90. Albanian male
91. An Albanian female

BULGARIA

92. Two Bulgarian girls

GREECE

93. Greek elder from Laconia
94. Girl from Attica
95. Female in national costume
96. Male showing Asian influence

CRETE

97. Elderly male from Crete

SOVIET UNION

98. "Great Russian" male
99. Blond White Russian female
100. Female Russian from Valogda
101. Ukrainian woman
102. Cossack from the Kuban
103. Group of Cossack males
104. Typical elder of the Caucasus region
105. Group of Avar males in national costume
106. Female from Volhynia revealing heavy Mongoloid influence
107. Ugrian-speaking female from Mari SSR

LAPPLAND

108. Lapp female
109. Lapp male

GYPSY

110. Spanish Gypsy woman

AN ANTHROPOLOGICAL OVERVIEW

Europe is a unique continent in having been the central location in which early Cro-Magnon fossil remains and Upper Paleolithic artifacts are found. We stress 'central' since these were not restricted to Europe, some finds having been located in adjacent areas of Western Asia and less clearly so in Northern Africa. Subsequent discoveries also indicate that some descendants of the Cro-Magnons moved eastwards across the Asian steppes, displacing earlier Neanderthal populations, and that the Upper Paleolithic culture associated with them eventually reached what is now Northern China, Korea and Japan.

What is remarkable about this fact is that the Cro-Magnons of thirty thousand years ago were essentially modern Europeans, and consequently it is less surprising that the Upper Paleolithic marks a revolutionary advance in the prehistory of culture and technology. The dramatic importance of this cultural revolution is symbolized by evidence which indicates that prior to the Upper Paleolithic, all the earlier forebears of man had dropped their refuse just wherever they were standing or sitting. By contrast, the Cro-Magnons lived in organized settlements, and carefully deposited their refuse — the remnants from their meals and often the chippings from their workshops — in refuse heaps, quite separate from their dwelling places. Indeed, the ghetto areas of contemporary West European and North American cities invite reflection in comparison with this early example of organized tidiness.

To briefly recap hominid evolutionary history, and to put these first modern Europeans in their true evolutionary perspective, it is necessary to recollect that in all probability our anthropoid ancestors formerly lived in the tropical and subtropical regions of the world still inhabited by monkeys and apes in this present day. Eventually, new species antecedent to man began to spread beyond the fertile tropical and subtropical lands which had nurtured them, where food was plentiful and easy to obtain, into more marginal terrain where greater intelligence and skill was required to secure sustenance. The changing ecological circumstances in which such migrant groups now found themselves seemingly exerted evolutionary selective pressures in favor of those qualities on which hominids relied for survival: intelligence being the most important of these.

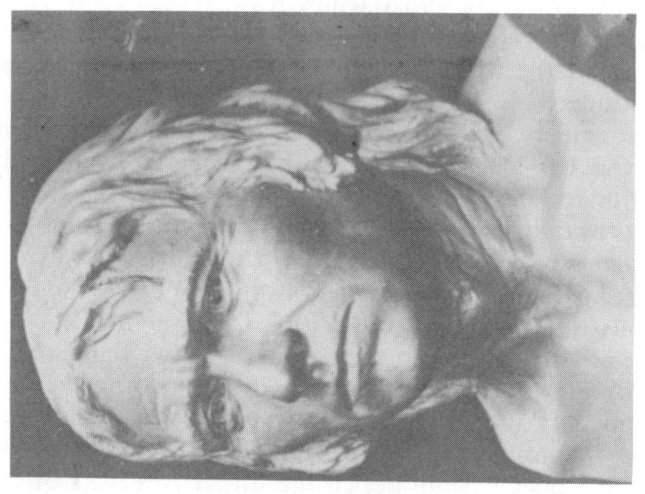
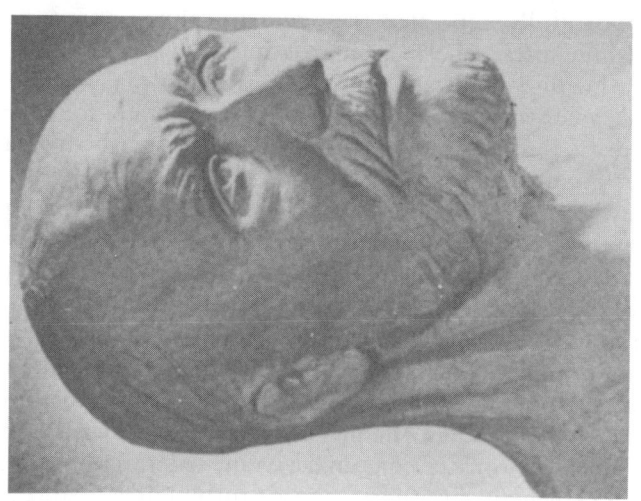

Reconstructed appearance of Cro-Magnon men – the earliest modern Europeans.

And so evolution progressed, through the *Homo erectus* level of 750,000 to 500,000 years ago, to Neanderthal man, the first *Homo sapiens* — so dubbed because individual Neanderthal characteristics and cultural achievements can be matched amongst sundry peoples and cultures which still survived in remote corners of the world as late as the Nineteenth Century.

The Neanderthals occupied Europe over a lengthy period, during the earlier part of which *Homo erectus* species still persisted in remote parts of the world, while in other areas the prevailing hominid stock rose to a comparable Neanderthaloid level (i.e. roughly parallel to or equivalent to the European Neanderthals). Then in Europe, and the adjacent lands of the Middle East, the Cro-Magnons, *Homo sapiens sapiens* — the first modern Europeans or 'Caucasoids' — appear suddenly in the fossil record. It is still disputed whether they evolved rapidly from Neanderthal stock (due to extremely strong selective pressure during the Fourth Ice Age) or whether they had been evolving separately for a much longer period, possibly in some area where subsequent glaciations or other natural conditions destroyed all or most of the evidence of their history. No matter which theory is correct, the Cro-Magnons supplanted the Neanderthals with astonishing rapidity in Europe, while elsewhere in the world Neanderthaloid populations remained generally in evidence, and Neanderthaloid levels of culture remained dominant.

Subsequent evidence traces the movement of Upper Paleolithic technology across Asia to the Far East, and the descendants of the Cro-Magnons undoubtedly spread into Northern Africa and over wide expanses of Asia during the ensuing Mesolithic, aided by their increasingly advanced technology and culture. Indeed it was this higher level of cultural achievement that made their expansion possible. Descendants of these same Cro-Magnons achieved settled communities in the favorable climate of the Balkans, Asia Minor, the Mediterranean and the "Fertile Crescent" in the sixth and fifth millennia B.C.

With the invention of agriculture, widening circles of technological achievement and migration disturbed large sections of the earth's population, as fresh movements of Cro-Magnon descended populations, often mixed in the areas of colonization with older stocks, continued their expansion back into the semi-tropical and into the tropical areas, there to mix with even older stocks, such as the Neanderthaloid 'Rhodesian Man', thus creating, through a numberless variety of different small gene pools, 'the living races of man.'

This ongoing turmoil of genetic amalgamation, genetic annihilation, selection and homogenization over the generations — all resulting from the expansion of Cro-Magnon descended populations from Western Eurasia and of (possibly not wholly unrelated) peoples from Eastern Asia — was primarily responsible for raising cultural levels in almost all parts of the world, and also, by genetic diffusion, transforming the remnants of the older regional stocks into the varied African, Asian and Amerindian peoples of today.

Equipped with a superior technology, the descendants of these first *Homo sapiens sapiens* continued to spread outwards from Mesolithic times down to the Nineteenth Century, but Europe in general remained one of the source areas of migration, and its population changed relatively slightly during all this time. Only a few incursions into Europe by non-European peoples occurred. There were the Turko-Tartar and Mongolian incursions into Eastern Europe, the North African settlement of Andalusia, Turkic incursions into the Balkans, and the general importation of slaves into Southern Europe during the the pan-mixia of the Imperial Roman period. But overall, the impact of non-European genes was not great — until the second half of the present century.

The first major 'backwash' of distinctly separate genetic forms into Europe began imperceptibly at first, following the vast wave of European sea-borne colonization and empire-building touched off by Columbus' discovery of the New World, and perhaps more importantly by Vasco da Gama's discovery of a sea route to the East round the southernmost tip of Africa. At first this brought only a small inflow of hybrid children, the offspring of the European colonists by native women. Because of the high cost of travel, and the high death rate among the European colonizers, such colored immigrants into Europe were relatively few, despite the fact that the Roman Catholic church actively encouraged inter-racial breeding as a method of spreading Christianity amongst the indigenous peoples of the conquered lands. However, even in Britain, the novelist Thackeray writes of the "ebony heiress," the daughter of a wealthy English sugar plantation owner in the

ANTHROPOLOGICAL OVERVIEW   13

Caribbean by a Negro mother, sent to London for education, who is courted by young Englishmen seeking financial gain. Yet it was only following the demolition of the worldwide European empires after the end of World War II, in the new spirit of 'anti-racism' and worldwide brotherhood, that the historic trend of outward migration from Europe came to an end, to be immediately replaced by a yet vaster flood of inward migration from the former colonial territories.

First, in the immediate decades following decolonization, came millions of Eurasians and Eurafricans, fearing in many cases to remain in the newly independent colonies in which they had been born. Indian Eurasians particularly flooded into Britain in uncounted numbers, where the younger Eurasians quickly sought English marriage partners to ensure acceptance in their new country of residence. Holland received enormous numbers of Dutch-Indonesians, who were not welcome in Indonesia. France became the target of settlement for millions of North Africans and Indo-Chinese of mixed origins, and Portugal, small in itself, was swamped by immigrants from its formerly widespread colonial territories. While this immigration at first went largely unnoticed, because most of the migrants were of at least partial European ancestry and keenly copied European customs in a search for identity, they were shortly to be followed by the now ongoing, and increasingly massive, influx of full-blooded Asian, African and West Indian peoples – political refugees, some of them, but mostly 'refugees from poverty' from the areas worst affected by the contemporary population explosion in the Third World. When we reflect that the population of India alone increases every six to seven days by the total population of Iceland, and every three months by the total population of Norway, and that African women in most sub-Saharan African countries average eight live births, while European women fail to average two live births, we can readily see that a continuation of the present flood of Afro-Asian immigration into Europe will mean the transformation beyond recognition of the Europe that we today know, within just a few generations.

Because the history of Europe has therefore become so fluid, we do not plan to structure this collection on traditional lines that seek to divide and identify clearly defined subraces in Europe. The geographical markers of such Weberian 'ideal types' — theoretical constructs of phenotypical extreme variation — have historically moved back and forth, but the enormity of genetic changes now accumulating as a result of vast inward migration from extra-European sources is such that the ancient Cro-Magnon type seems threatened with eventual extinction in its characteristic and 'pure' European form. We have thus decided to follow the precedent of the renowned pioneer anthropologist, John Beddoe, who — faced with a similar but infinitely smaller pattern of change at a purely local level by increasing internal migration within England — decided that it was important to record the traditional population as it then was, before inter-county distinctions were completely obliterated. In a poignant explanation, in the introduction to his admirable survey entitled *The Races of Britain*, published first in 1885 (Cliveden Press, 1983), Beddoe stated that: "The ever-increasing rapidity of local migration and intermixture (of British peoples within Britain), due to the extension of railways and the altered conditions of society, will in the next generations inextricably confuse the limits and proportions of the British races; and it is a source of satisfaction to me that I have labored to observe and record phenomena, which however trivial they may appear from some points of view, may for generations to come retain some biological and historical value." Little could he envisage the situation that confronts the student of European anthropology today!

Ignoring, then, any effort to record the anthropology of the recent immigrants into Europe, notwithstanding their vast numbers and high fertility rate (it is projected, for example, that by the next generation the number of non-French schoolchildren in French schools will outnumber those of French descent), we will present portraits of the indigenous population of Europe as it was during the first half of this century. That being the limit of our objective, we may summarize the anthropological history of Europe as follows. The European peoples are the direct descendants of the original Cro-Magnons. Until the second half of this century, immigration into Europe was relatively small, the main flow of population having been out of Europe from Mesolithic (and perhaps Upper Paleolithic) times onwards, culminating in a vast flow of overseas colonization and empire building in the centuries which followed Columbus' discovery of the Americas and Vasco da Gama's epic

ANTHROPOLOGICAL OVERVIEW 15

voyage around the Cape of Good Hope. In general, the Northern or Germanic peoples have been the most protected (in Europe) from genetic modification by exposure to non-European peoples, except for minor contact with the Lapps of the Arctic circle. The Mediterranean peoples, frequently reinforced by migrations from Central and Northern Europe — e.g. by the arrival of the early Greeks, the Latins, the Celts, and the Germanic Franks, Goths, Vandals, Lombards and Normans — were essentially similar to the peoples of Northern Europe, despite their slightly heavier pigmentation. Local variations are found, such as are represented by the Basque and Dinaric strains, representing ancient local variants, but in general the ancient Mediterranean stock has retained its early genetic identity quite clearly, especially in the rural areas, despite substantial imports of population into Southern Europe from the Middle East and North Africa in the Roman period. Similarly, Central Europe and isolated areas reveal signs of the genetic survival of a broader-headed Cro-Magnon variety (like all widely-spread populations, the Cro-Magnons revealed local variations in type), but Southern Spain was significantly influenced by Moorish occupation over several centuries. Gypsy influence in Europe has been slight, but Jewish influence substantial. Parts of the Balkans, such as Macedonia and Greece, have been dramatically influenced by Turkish and other West Asian influences, and the eastern or Asian frontier of Europe, which lies within the Soviet Union, has a complex genetic history. Some large populations, such as the Russians and the Ukrainians, have retained their identity quite markedly, and small groups among populations such as the Avars and Cossacks have also preserved a relatively distinct genetic identity. On the other hand, many southern Soviet populations result from a very complex amalgam, including considerable Turko-Tartar influence. In particular, Georgia, the land from which Stalin derived, is marked by a strong Armenoid strain which links it historically and anthropologically with southeastern Asia Minor, even though it technically falls within the boundaries of geographic Europe.

Let us conclude this brief introduction by saying that we hope that those who peruse this text will find some value in a collation of anthropological portraits which though not uncommon in themselves are too infrequently arranged in any systematic geographical pattern. They represent the traditional appearance of a continent whose population, after some thirty thousand years of continuity, now seems certain to be transformed out of recognition within the next two generations.

Fig. 1 Although Neolithic England may have been inhabited by an Atlanto-Mediterranean type population somewhat akin to modern Mediterranean peoples, it was subsequently settled by a more northern European type, notably the Celts, who had expanded westwards from an earlier homeland in what is today Bavaria and Switzerland. The Celts were then largely supplanted by waves of West Germans. Most of England acquired an "Anglo-Saxon" or West German character between the fifth and tenth centuries. The family name of this Englishman was of Saxon provenance.

Fig. 2 The Angles and Saxons originated in northwestern Germany, but in the ninth and tenth centuries their invasions were followed by a massive settlement, particularly in the East and North, of North Germans of Danish and Norwegian extraction — the Vikings. East Anglia, Lincolnshire, Yorkshire and Northern England, the lowlands of Scotland, and coastal sections in many areas were occupied by Vikings. Where Anglo-Saxons remained, the two closely related peoples soon intermixed. Portrayed above is the well-known English poet, Rupert Brook.

ENGLAND

Fig. 3 Viking settlement was heaviest in the North. This illustration portrays a Yorkshireman, with the features that through the centuries have come to be associated with England, and particularly with the landowning class. In recent years, however, the slow influence of intermarriage as a result of colonial adventures in non-White lands around the world, the periodic immigration of refugees from Europe in times of disturbance (as of Jews from Germany, Poland and Russia), and recently an increasingly massive immigration of Asians and Africans has made the original English type almost rare in modern England. The subject of this picture died in World War I without offspring.

Fig. 4 Light coloring of hair and eyes has steadily decreased in England in this century, due to the changing population resulting from emigration as well as immigration, but English children of recently unmixed descent still tend to have light hair when young, which may turn darker into adulthood.

SCOTLAND 21

Fig. 5 The lowlands and southern uplands of Scotland were heavily settled by Anglo-Saxons and then by Vikings. Consequently lowland Scotland became one of the most clearly Germanic parts of the British Isles, its characteristic population differing but little from that of Northern England, despite the terrible border warfare and bloodletting which wracked English and Scottish history for centuries. Scottish regiments earned fame in the British army once the two countries were united. Shown here is J. R. H. Anderson of Ayrshire. Only the major Scottish cities have so far been penetrated by non-European immigrant people.

Fig. 6 Although the Scottish Highlands are traditionally regarded as Celtic, the Celts were not greatly different in appearance from the Germanic peoples, from whom they may have become separated as a distinct population as little as four to five thousand years ago. Furthermore, parts of the Scottish Highlands and Western Isles were actually settled by Vikings, who adopted many Celtic customs in their new homeland. Our illustration portrays an officer of the Argyle and Sutherland Highland Regiment. Today the Scottish Highlands are sadly depopulated.

WALES

Fig. 7 Elements of the pre-Celtic population of the British Isles were absorbed by the Celts, who primarily established themselves as a ruling caste, and this may have been particularly the case in the areas of mountain and marsh refuge, which in turn became survival areas for the Celts following the Germanic invasions of the British (Brythonic Celtic) Isles. Wales (the land of the *Wealas*, or 'foreigners' as the Anglo-Saxons called them) and West Wales, or Cornwall, were areas where the Cymric (Celtic) language and culture survived. Our subject lived in Merionethshire. Because of regional unemployment, only a few major Welsh cities have become centers for Asian and African immigration.

Fig. 8 Ireland was another area of Celtic (mixed with some pre-Celtic) survival. However, its history is not simple. Vikings founded the major coastal cities of Ireland, and Norman and English repeatedly invaded and eventually gained control of the island. Represented here is an Anglo-Irishman, a descendant of these Anglo-Norman invaders. The Anglo-Irish tended to be a landowning military class, and provided a remarkably high percentage of the senior British Army officers, just as the Prussian families served as a gene pool for the German Army officer corps. The independence of Ireland in this century has led to the emigration of many of the Anglo-Irish families to diverse parts of the world, thus breaking up this distinctive gene pool with its military associations.

IRELAND

Fig. 9 The Celtic Irish element is well represented by this old lady from Dooley, in County Clare on the Western coast of Ireland. Irish or Gaelic speaking Celts represented an earlier wave of Celtic invasion than the Brythonic or British Celts of Wales and Cornwall. Irish Celts, known as "Scotti" or "raiders," subsequently invaded the mountainous highlands of "Scotland," giving that country its name and bringing the Celtic language to the Scottish Highlands.

Fig. 10 The close similarity of features linking the Celts and the Germans, both historically and in living populations, can be seen in this photograph of an elderly Irish woman from the West of County Kerry, a stronghold of Celtic survival. The depressed economy of Ireland has discouraged the present wave of Afro-Asian immigration, so marked in England, but a few Chinese and Indian families are now to be found in every town, gaining a foothold by way of the restaurant business.

Fig. 11 Possibly the 'purest' areas of Celtic survival are in the *Gaeltach* or western fringe of Ireland, where Irish (Goidelic Celtic) is still spoken. Pictured above is an Aran Islander, whose blue eyes and dark hair, regarded by many as a uniquely Irish combination, may reflect Celtic and pre-Celtic admixture. According to the Romans, the Celts were red-headed and blue eyed, while the Germans were blond haired and blue eyed. Both Celts and Germans shared similar facial features.

Fig. 12 The Faeroe Isles, situated midway between Norway, Iceland and the British Isles, were settled solely by Vikings, mainly from Norway. Their small population of under 30,000 men, women and children, retains the genetic identity and physical appearance of the Vikings of a thousand years ago.

IRELAND

Fig. 13 Closest to the Irish are the Icelanders. Just as Ireland was settled by Celts and subsequently by Vikings, so Iceland was settled by Vikings from Norway, with a subsequent admixture of Irish. This child could as likely be imagined in an Irish or English scene, though his extreme fairness reflects his Icelandic heritage, which remains today more blond due to its relative isolation from immigration since the eleventh century. Although Iceland is the oldest democracy in Europe, it has a population of only a quarter of a million.

Fig. 14 The coasts of Norway, a mountainous and dramatically beautiful land, are warmed by the gulf stream, thus making the coastal valleys and fjords attractive to settlers despite its northerly latitude. To this day Norway retains much of its original North Germanic heritage, despite efforts to encourage the immigration of Turkish, Vietnamese Asians and other non-European settlers, which has been facilitated by the industrial development of North Sea oil. Our illustration portrays Odd Nansen, the renowned humanist and nationalist, who did much to help organize relief for the great Russian famine, brought on by the Bolshevik revolution.

Fig. 15 This young Norwegian woman from Bergen in Hordaland typifies the classic beauty for which Norwegian and Swedish women are renowned. Genetically, this is the product of hundreds of generations of selection and inbreeding, which is unlikely to survive the current trend towards the introduction of more heterogeneous and markedly different peoples into the Scandinavian gene pool.

Fig. 16 Until the discovery of oil, fishing in the warm coastal waters of Norway had been a prime base for the Norwegian economy for thousands of years. Pictured above is Johan Hjort, who was responsible for training a staff of scientists to study the breeding patterns and ecological needs of the shoals of fish which were the basis of the Norwegian fishing industry. North Sea oil, however, has threatened the stability of the fishing industry, as have modern electronically equipped fishing boats, which tend to sweep the seas empty. Over-fishing is negating Johan Hjort's work, and depopulating the coastal villages in which the old Viking population had retained its historic gene pools.

Fig. 17 Leif Larsen, Lt. Commander in the Norwegian Navy, was well-known for his commando skills. Until recently, Norway maintained one of the largest merchant marines in the world, enabling its young men to continue to take to the seas which had been so beloved of their forebears.

Fig. 18 Not all modern Swedish women retain the classic 'Nordic' features of this young woman, which were once almost universal, since immigration has become a reality in Sweden today, and young Swedes are often romantically attracted by Asian and African visitors. Furthermore, the more socially attractive an individual, the higher the possibility, in modern Sweden, that the allures of social life will win out over the quieter pleasures of raising a family.

SWEDEN

Fig. 19 Scandinavian or Nordic peoples typically are light skinned, fair haired and fair eyed. However, the head form varies slightly, due to the survival in some mountain valleys of traces of an ancient broader-headed variant. This individual from Sodermanland, near Stockholm, reveals an extreme dolichocephaly or long-headedness, which in less pronounced form is more characteristic of Norwegians and Swedes in general, and reflects the classic proto-Celtic and proto-Germanic Hallstatt Iron Age type.

Fig. 20 King Gustav VI, pictured here, was representative of many Swedish men of his age. Although the royal family of Sweden is descended from one of Napoleon's marshals, this resemblance is due to the custom whereby North European royalty habitually married into other royal families of Germanic provenance, hence the 'Swedish' appearance.

SWEDEN

Fig. 21 Another example of the classic Swedish 'Nordic' look — typified by clearcut features, a straight nose, high forehead, well-defined chin, a relatively long head, and light skin, eyes and hair.

Fig. 22 Situated strategically to the South of Norway and Sweden, at the mouth of the Baltic sea, Denmark has historically been a prime center for Nordic culture and innovation. Historically the Danes lived in southern Sweden, but the old Danish area was incorporated into Sweden by force due to its geopolitical situation, and thus the present day Danes are largely of closely related Jutish descent. Post-World War II Denmark has an ever-increasing population of non-European character. Pictured here is a young Danish girl from the rural district of Lyoe. As is common, the immigrant populations have located, initially at least, in the cities, where their genetic impact tends to be geographically restricted to infiltration of the large urban populations, and is slow in finding its way into rural areas.

GERMANY

Fig. 23 The ancestors of the Angles, Saxons, Jutes and Danes who settled England came from North Germany and Schleswig-Holstein, a province which borders Germany and Jutland. Our subject comes from this vital North German area — which two thousand years ago was also a part of the nucleus from which many of the more southerly German populations of today originated — and typifies the "West German" type very clearly. Frisians, a people who extended historically along the German North Sea coast into the northern part of the Netherlands, are of a similar type. Those who know England would not be surprised to see this man in an English village.

Fig. 24 Small areas in North Germany, which were formerly marshland, reveal genetic traces of an older European population which was characterized by slightly broader heads than modern North Germans. Carleton Coon identified these as "Borreby" variants, after skeletal remains discovered at a site bearing that name. Here we see a North German lighthouse keeper, with a somewhat Borreby roundness of face, preparing the ancient pagan Yuletide tree for the winter festival of that name.

GERMANY

Fig. 25 Berlin, once the proud capital of Prussia, formerly lay in the center of Germany. Territorial losses following World War I, and more especially World War II, converted Eastern Germany into Polish territory, and Central Germany into Soviet-dominated "East Germany," with Berlin a divided city in the center of "East Germany." In recent years, numbers of youths of all races, devotees of the 'alternative' life style, have moved to Berlin, taking advantage of its delicate political situation surrounded by Communist military. But a substantial German stock remains, as witnessed by these two girls photographed on a Berlin street.

Fig. 26 Another German street scene which presents a typical cross-section of the traditional German population. However, the last few decades have seen the major German cities acquire large populations of immigrant Turkish and North African 'guest-workers,' who now seek to become permanent residents.

GERMANY

Fig. 27 Just as the Anglo-Irish landowners provided a prominent element in the officer corps of the British Army, so the large German landowners, descended from the Teutonic knights who conquered Prussia, provided a tightly knit gene pool of "Junkers" who, generation after generation, supplied much of the officer class for the Prussian and subsequently the German armed forces. After suffering heavy losses in World War I and again in World War II, Prussia was overrun by the Soviets who massacred many of the members of the landowning families that remained. The subsequent worldwide dispersal of surviving elements, meant that the "Junkers," as portrayed above, no longer survive as a genetic entity.

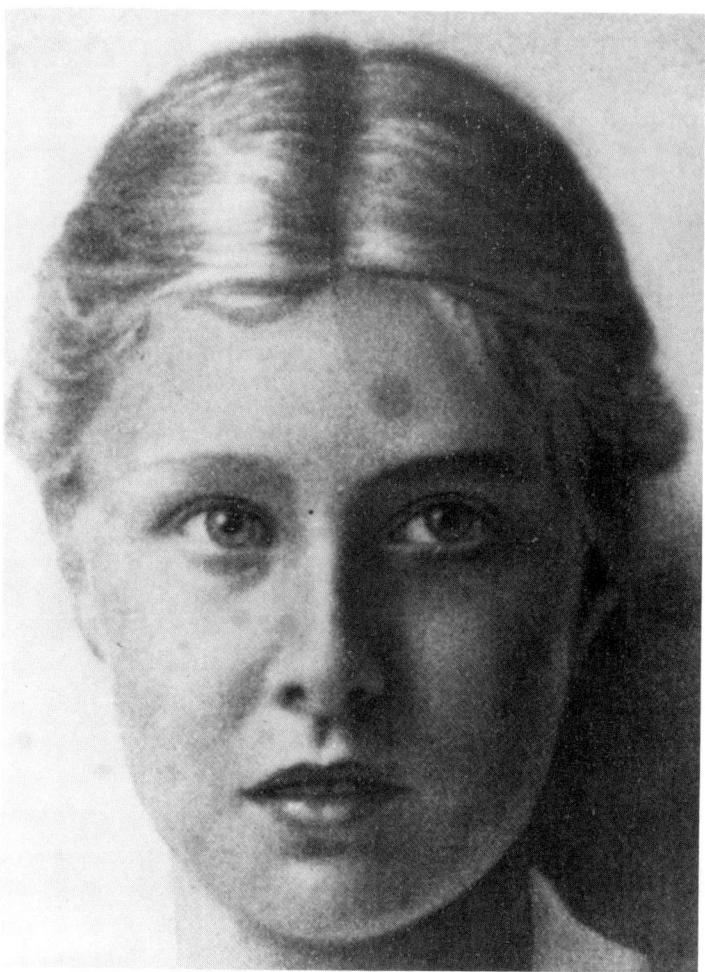

Fig. 28 Silesia was another ancient German land from which the Germans were driven out after World War II. Pictured above is a young Silesian German. Those Silesian Germans who survived World War II's brutal expulsion by Soviet forces, and the general slaughter on the Eastern Front, are today dispersed throughout West Germany, with a small percentage in East Germany.

GERMANY 45

Fig. 29 Bavaria was an area of relatively late Germanic settlement, and some of the mountain valleys still reveal the influence of older broader-headed and heavier-pigmented Alpine peoples. Yet in the course of history Bavaria became proudly German, being settled, as the Germans like to joke, by the "poor walkers" who did not try to traverse the mountains of Switzerland to settle the sunny lands of Italy. Here portrayed is a young Bavarian family at home.

Fig. 30 Adjacent to the Bavarian plains are many small populations, German in name and culture, but somewhat variant in physical type. This lady is from the Allgau, and is pictured in traditional nineteenth century Allgau costume.

AUSTRIA

Fig 31 Medieval German knights introduced German culture and established flourishing German settlements in many lands which were Celtic or Slavic prior to the Middle Ages. They established German kingdoms and principalities in what is now Czechoslovakia and settled Austria thoroughly, laying the foundation for the powerful and long-lasting German-led Austro-Hungarian empire. Austria, or Osterreich, literally means "the Eastern Kingdom." Pictured here is an officer of the Austrian Army. The facial resemblance to English and Anglo-Irish military leaders, such as Montgomery, Auchinleck and Wavell, is quite remarkable.

Fig. 32 The Netherlands are historically nothing other than "the lowlands" of German settlement. While the Frisians may claim a separate Germanic identity of great antiquity, various Germanic peoples, notably the Saxons and Franks, dominated the province of Holland for many centuries, and with the exception of a few Borreby-type strains surviving in the low, formerly marshy areas at the mouth of the Rhine, the Dutch (=Deutsch) are Germans pure and simple. Portrayed here is a girl from North Holland. More than most other West European countries, Holland has accepted immigrants from its former colonies, so that the Dutch cities today have very large colonies of Indonesian and other immigrants, of both pure and mixed Asian and African descent.

BELGIUM

Fig. 33 Belgium is not an historical entity but was created as a buffer state to halt French expansion into the low countries, always a prosperous and dynamic area. Deriving its name, somewhat artificially, from the ancient (Brythonic) Celtic Belgae, its inhabitants are divided between the French-speaking Walloons, and the Germanic-speaking Flemings. Here we see portrayed a Flemish Belgian, notably Maurice Maeterlinck, a poet renowned for his ability to introduce the spirit of ancient fairy tales and folklore into modern life situations.

MODERN EUROPE

Fig. 34 Returning to geographical Scandinavia, we portray here a Finnish politician, Kalevi Sorsa. The Finns may represent the survivors of a non-Germanic, and indeed non-Indo-European population, that formerly occupied all the lands around the Baltic as hunters and fishers, but were driven out by Germanic cultivators to the West, and by Indo-European Latvians, Lithuanians, Prussians and Slavs to the East. Related to the Estonians, the Finns kept their Finno-Ugric language, despite substantial Swedish influence — and a large portion of the present-day Finnish population, settled around Abo, is actually Swedish by descent and culture. Genetically the Finns are probably heavily influenced from their North Germanic neighbors, whom they to some extent resemble — in a sharp physical contrast to the reindeer-herding Lapps of the far north (see Fig. 108 and 109).

FINLAND

Fig. 35 These young Finns exemplify the small and widely dispersed, closely inbreeding population of Finland. Intelligent and dynamic, the Finns are an impressive and creative people. Genetically, these small and isolated village settlements have preserved the archaetypal pattern of human breeding and evolutionary process. Harmful recessive genes surface quickly and, where deleterious, tend to be isolated and bred out of the population — thus keeping the surviving stock free from excessive genetic load.

Fig. 36 Despite the sharp linguistic contrast, modern Estonians, like Finns, do not differ in appearance as greatly from the North German peoples as might be expected. From Viking times, the entire east Baltic area was heavily infiltrated by Swedish peoples. The East Baltic face may tend towards a roundness, with less sharp features than those of North Germanic or Scandinavian peoples, but otherwise there are many points of at least superficial resemblance, as portrayed in this photograph of an Estonian peasant.

ESTONIA

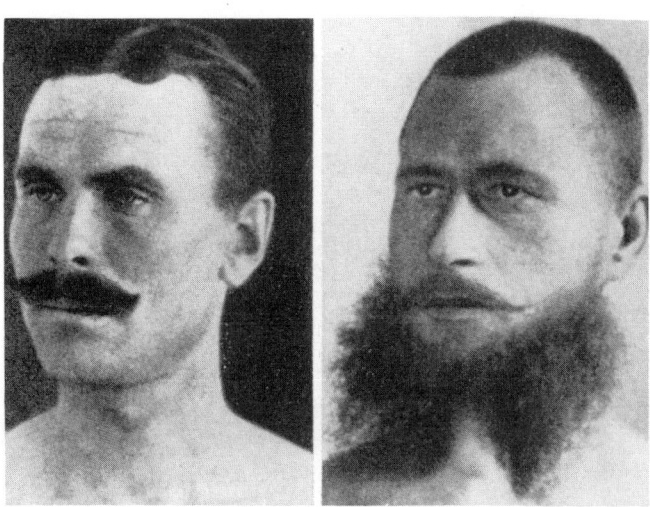

Fig. 37 Neighbors of the Estonians, the Latvians speak a language — despite Soviet attempts (since they seized Latvia during World War II) to substitute the Sovietized Russian language — which belongs to the Baltic group of Indo-Germanic languages. Again we find a substantial Swedish influence over the past thousand years, but there is an underlying element, parallel to that in Estonia, which resulted in a physical type that is sometimes called "East Baltic." Blondness, often of a flaxen variety, is widespread, but features are more rounded than those of the Germanic peoples. The ethnic history of the Baltic peoples would seem to indicate an initial colonization by Baltic-speaking Indo-European peoples — resulting in some admixture with Finno-Ugric survivors — followed by subsequent infusions of Scandinavian blood, via Swedish trading settlements.

Fig. 38 While Latvians reveal the "East Baltic" variant rather clearly, the Lithuanians appear more akin to the Swedish type. This group of young Lithuanian women and girls well portrays the ethnic type. South of Lithuania, the land was formerly settled by another East Baltic people, the Prussians, but the Prussian language and ethnic identity disappeared after its conquest by the Teutonic knights and its absorption into Germanic Europe.

FRANCE

Fig. 39 France has an extremely complex anthropological history. The Western seacoast of this rich and wonderful land was probably formerly occupied by an Atlanto-Mediterranean type, akin to the ancient peoples of Iberia and the pre-Bronze Age British Isles. Inland it was populated by a broad-headed Alpine people, with a Mediterranean-type population along its southern shores. Around three thousand years ago France was overrun by the Celts, and thus acquired the name of Gaul, as used by the Romans. Following the collapse of the Roman empire under pressure from the Germanic Goths, Vandals and other Germanic nations, northern and eventually southern France was conquered by the Germanic Franks, who established themselves as a ruling class, the progenitors of French aristocracy, as represented by the Comte d'Aulnay, above. The modern name France derives from the kingdom of the Franks.

Fig. 40 In some areas, particularly the North, the Franks settled in large numbers, and consequently changed the local population in a more Germanic direction. Other areas, such as Normandy, were settled by Viking Northmen, thus confirming the Germanic appearance which is still evident in the population of Normandy to this day. Yet other areas reveal a blending of Frankish German with Alpine. The lady portrayed here indicates the survival of genetic components from the broad-headed pre-Celtic Alpine stock.

Fig. 41 The central 'massif' region of France is home to another variant, sometimes described as Dinaric, whose origins are difficult to identify. Our subject is a miner, who differs clearly from the broad-headed lady in Figure 40, and again from the aristocratic Frankish-type illustrated in Fig. 39. Like the other nations of Western Europe, especially those which had overseas empires, the French cities have experienced an influx of millions of non-Europeans, mostly from North Africa, but actually from all parts of the former French empire. Other territories, as in the West Indies, are regarded as overseas departments of France — with freedom of movement and migration.

Fig. 42 One of the more romantic divisions of France is Brittany, which still preserves its own Brythonic Celtic language. The Bretons are not direct survivors of the older Celtic population of Caesar's Gaul. The latter were Gaelic Celts, as the name Gaul implies, while the Bretons are Brythonic Celts related to Welsh and Cornish people. As the Saxons swept into Britain, some Britons migrated across the sea to northwest Gaul, where they established Brittany. Two Breton counties bear names reminding us of their earlier homeland in Britain, where Devon and Cornwall still survive as modern counties.

FRANCE

Fig. 43 This Breton matron may reflect a pre-Celtic genetic survival from the Atlanto-Mediterranean population that occupied Brittany before the arrival of the Celts from Britain. The Celts, like the Germans, were slave-owning peoples, and older populations were frequently enslaved after Celtic conquest. Some central European Alpine elements may also have survived in the Breton highlands, as this portrait suggests.

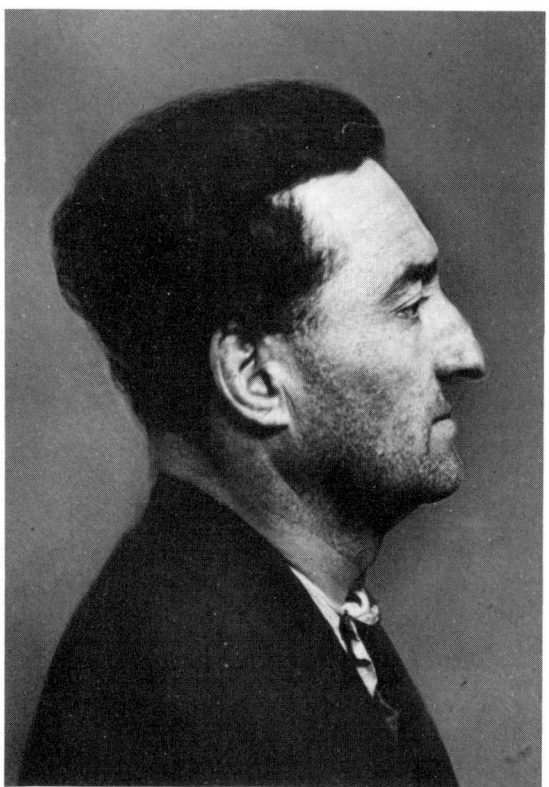

Fig. 44 Aquitaine and the Pyrenees were home to a pre-Celtic population which spoke a totally non-Indo-European language, namely Basque. This Frenchman lives in the Pyrenees, and represents a pre-Celtic, pre-Frankish element. Although Aquitaine was conquered by the Franks, they settled it but thinly as major landowners, and the countryside retained a substantial Basque component. The Basques of southeastern France are generally regarded as being more pure than those of the larger Spanish Basque lands.

Fig. 45 The main center of Basque speech today is in northeastern Spain, and Basque nationalist consciousness is high in this area. The Basque population differs in blood group characteristics markedly from other European peoples, and the high incidence of group Rh Negative in Western Europe is believed to be due to their genetic influence.

Fig. 46 Like France, Spain has a very complex ethnic history. Formerly occupied by a Neolithic Atlanto-Mediterranean population, it was largely settled by the Celts, before being conquered by the Romans. Following the collapse of Roman power, Spain was divided into Visigothic kingdoms, and saw the passage of the Germanic Vandals on their way through the conquer North Africa. Later, Islamicized North Africans and Arabs conquered much of the peninsula and established themselves securely for many centuries in southern Spain. Consequently the Spanish physical type varies widely according to region, while the aristocracy remained largely Germanic in provenance. Portrayed above is a Spaniard from Salamanca.

SPAIN

Fig. 47 Even in medieval times, Spanish beauty was portrayed as generally Mediterranean in type, although amongst the nobility a more blond Visigothic type survived. This Spanish woman may reflect Moorish genes, but would not conflict with an Elizabethan Englishman's concept of Spanish feminine beauty.

Fig. 48 The Balearic Isles are regarded as Spanish, and this group of Balearic women reveals a fairly accurate picture of the ethnic variations that may also be found on the mainland. Only in Andalusia, in the South of Spain, do we find the very dark, North African type, a legacy of centuries of Islamic occupation.

PORTUGAL

Fig. 49 Portugal, like Spain, experienced periods of Atlanto-Mediterranean, Celtic and Visigothic domination. Facing the Atlantic, its people became competent fishing and sailing folk, and it was Portugal that pioneered the seagoing and empire building proclivities of the West European nations. Being Catholic by religion, however, substantial genetic admixture with the peoples of Asia, Africa and South America resulted from their establishment of overseas colonies, some of which found its way back to Portugal. Here portrayed are two Portuguese fishermen.

Fig. 50 Today many hybrid refugees from former Portuguese colonies have retreated to Portugal, where there is quite a sharp division between the older stock, only slightly mixed with colonial peoples, and the more recent post-World War II influx of non-European peoples. This rural Portuguese girl shows little evidence of non-European genetic admixture, and probably resembles the Portuguese of the fifteenth and sixteenth centuries, who conducted wide ranging maritime explorations before other European nations had even considered the possibility of intercontinental exploration by sea.

Fig. 51 Switzerland is another ethnically complex country, unified by its mountainous terrain and its determination to preserve local freedoms. The western part of Switzerland speaks French, as would this girl from the Jura mountains adjacent to the French border.

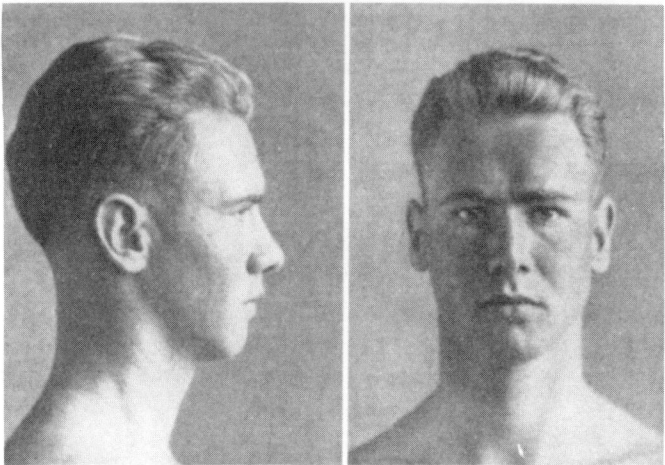

Fig. 52 By contrast, most of Switzerland is German-speaking, like the occupants of the ancient city of Basle, where this young man was photographed.

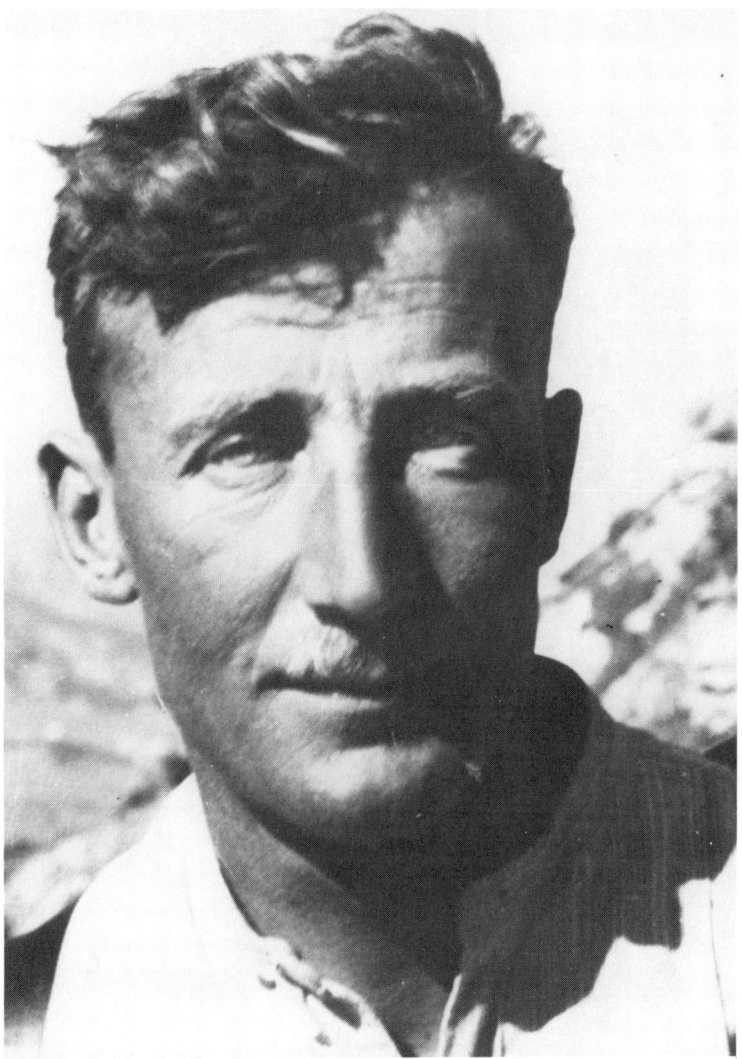

Fig. 53 Virtually all the major Alpine valleys on the northern slopes of the Alps are German-speaking, This guide, who lives in the Engadine, is typically Germanic in appearance, as are most German-speaking Swiss in the larger valleys.

Fig. 54 Southern Switzerland is Italian-speaking, and genetically linked to various Italian residual populations. Portrayed above are two Italian Swiss women from Valois, who reflect 'Alpine' genetic traits.

ITALY   71

Fig. 55 Italy was historically protected from the rest of Europe by the Alps, but the major passes saw the passage of many armies of conquest. Smaller valleys served as places of refuge for older populations, being largely untouched as the invaders poured through to plunder and settle the rich plains of northern Italy. The Dolomites, home to this woman, has many such valleys. There the ethnic relationship is with Yugoslavia.

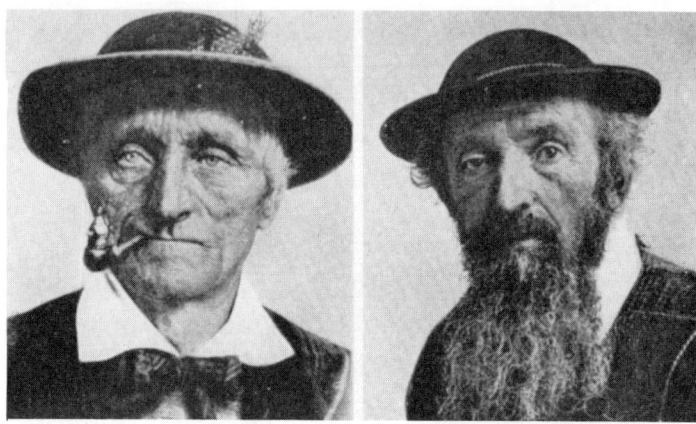

Fig. 56 The Italian Tyrol is a major area of dispute, having been purely German-speaking until World War I allowed the victors to assign this South Alpine part of Austria to the Italians as one of the spoils of war. Despite an Italian government policy, whereby Italians from the overpopulated south of Italy have been settled in the Tyrol, the countryside remains strongly German. Portrayed here are German-speaking Tyroleans of an older generation.

ITALY

Fig. 57 Piedmont, formerly a separate kingdom, is also distinctly 'northern' in its character, as this illustration of a Piedmontese from Lanzo reveals.

MODERN EUROPE

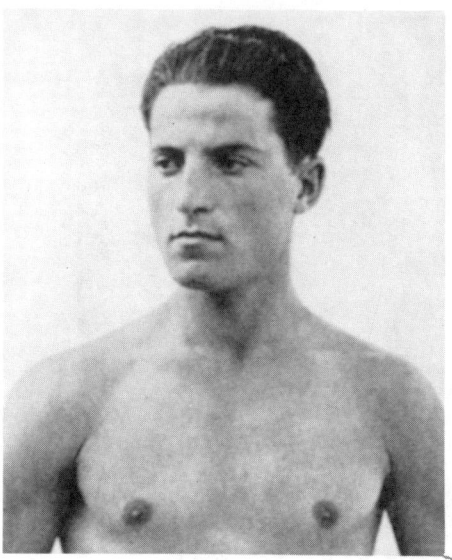

Fig. 58 Northern Italy, once the home of the ancestors of the Romans and Italic peoples, and later of Celts, was settled by Germanic Lombards following the collapse of Rome. Despite migration into the major industrial cities from the south, and from outside Europe, the north Italian towns and countryside retains something of its Germanic ethnic component. Portrayed here is a subject from Verona.

Fig. 59 The ancient character of "Italic" Italy, as also represented by the Romans of the Republican period, is still to be seen in this inhabitant of the Tiber Valley, the center of final Latin settlement and the site of Rome itself.

Fig. 60 This young girl from central Italy illustrates the graduation of physical type from Nordic to Mediterranean as one travels from north to south in Italy.

ITALY

Fig. 61 Naples has always been a somewhat cosmopolitan town, and different in many ways from the surrounding countryside. This male from Naples compares with the Basque shown in Fig. 44, and may derive genes from an ancient pre-Indo-European population.

Fig. 62 South of Naples we enter Calabria, one of the oldest areas of Neolithic civilization, much influenced, also, by settlers from Ancient Greece. The typical Calabrian rural type is well represented in this photograph.

ITALY

Fig. 63 The homogeneity of the Calabrian population is demonstrated by comparing this young Calabrian with the somewhat older woman portrayed in the previous illustration. Both would be regarded as typical of the Mediterranean type, believed to have formerly extended from the Atlantic to the Levant.

MODERN EUROPE

Fig. 64 Also Mediterranean in type are the inhabitants of Sardinia. This girl may be compared with the young men portrayed in Fig. 65. The Sardinians may be one of the best surviving representatives of the original circum-Mediterranean population of the Neolithic.

ITALY

Fig. 65 A group of young Sardinian males who demonstrate a remarkable similarity of appearance, due to a high level of local inbreeding over two or more thousand years.

Fig. 66 Moving to the Slavic world, we find in Poland a people who may have become partially Slav and partially Germanic during the two thousand years or more that Germans and Slavs have warred over boundaries in this central European region.

Fig. 67 Blood group analysis does not show any immediate break in physical type as one moves eastwards from Germany into Slavic Europe, but facial changes do become obvious. Few would place these round-faced Polish children in a German setting, even though their pigmentation and blood group patterns are not very different.

Fig. 68 This Polish game warden, who has just killed a wild lynx (an animal which enjoys some degree of protection), reveals the broader-headed and rounder-faced qualities which often distinguish Poles, though this is not a characteristic of the Slavic peoples in general.

POLAND

Fig. 69 Once again, these two young men are more easily placed in Poland than further westwards on the North European plain which Poles share with their German neighbors to the West.

Fig. 70 To the south, Poland verges on the Carpathians, and here different varieties and local variations in population are to be found. These Ruthenian Carpathian dwellers have been partially protected from external genetic influences by their mountains and valleys, and can be likened with difficulty to other mountain dwellers in the same range, and even less readily to the Poles living on the plains to their north. They are generally described as being of Dinaric type, with some Alpine influence. Known as the "Goral" or 'mountaineers' the Ruthenians appear to be descended from early Slavs who admixed in the mountains with an older broad-headed Dinaric population.

CZECHOSLOVAKIA

Fig. 71 Czechoslovakia is a composite state, created following the break-up of the Austro-Hungarian and the German empire after World War I. The boundaries of Czechoslovakia were drawn along the mountain crests, leaving many "Sudeten" Germans inside the new Slavic state, cut off from other German lands. Czechoslovakia comprises a variety of Slavic peoples, who had formerly been ruled by German nobles for many centuries. This young Czech girl reveals fair coloring and a round, happy face.

Fig. 72 Moravia was one of the major Slavic-speaking provinces which were incorporated in the newly-created Czechoslovakia after World War I. With Bohemia it is the main center of Czech settlement. Czechs are to be distinguished from the Slovaks of Slovakia by their more Nordic appearance although in general both provinces show a drift towards broader-headed character during the Christian period. In general Czechs are somewhat similar to the southern Germans of Bavaria.

Fig. 73 Of the diverse Czech nationalities, Slovaks, who inhabit the mountainous district of Slovakia situated between Moravia and Ruthenia, are broader-headed and more Dinaric in profile, suggesting the absorption of an older population by the Slavic settlers.

Fig. 74 Bohemia was always one of the more colorful parts of central Europe. Today it is the major province of Czechoslovakia, in which the beautiful and historic (though primarily German in creation) city of Prague stands. Czechs differ from the West Russian Slavs in their stronger profiles and straighter noses. Like the Wends of old, they may represent considerable Germanic genetic admixture.

Fig. 75 A Vlach of Czechoslovakia in national costume. The term Vlach, derives from a Slavic word which is cognate with the Anglo-Saxon "Wealas," simply 'foreigner.' It appears to have been used in all areas of southerly Slavic movement to refer to any pre-existing population, and Vlachs are found in Romania, Bulgaria, Yugoslavia and even Greece. They are distinguished by a generally Dinaric cast of features, and predate Roman, Gothic, Slavic, Ugrian, Avar, and Bulgar migrations.

Fig. 76 Hungary was once the center of Attila's short-lived European empire, but after his defeat and death the Huns dispersed and returned to their Asian steppeland home. The Hungarian language of the present-day is related to Finnish, Estonian and the Ugric languages, entered Europe as a result of a later migration of the Magyar, also from the Asian steppes. Despite the ensuing centuries, some traces of Mongoloid genes survive, marking off certain individuals in the Hungarian population from their more characteristically European neighbors.

HUNGARY

Fig. 77 Although the Huns settled the middle Danubian region temporarily, they left few traces, and Hungarians actually speak a Magyar language derived from a later intrusion into Europe of related Asian peoples. However, Celtic, Ostrogothic and subsequent Germanic immigration has given most present-day Hungarians a characteristically European appearance, as evidenced by these two Hungarian girls.

Fig. 78 Romania was once an important Roman province and Latin survived to become the basis of the modern Romanian language. However, the original population has been overrun by many peoples, and was the center of the Ostrogothic kingdom for several generations. These young Hungarian men are from Bukovina in the Carpathian mountains.

Fig. 79 A Romanian from Tulcea, illustrating a somewhat more Mediterranean type than the young men portrayed in Fig. 78. Tulcea is situated close to the Black Sea, in the lowlands of Dobruja.

Fig. 80 Transylvania (formerly a part of Dacia and Thracian in population) has retained a variety of distinctive populations, ranging from Romanian to German and Magyar speaking minorities, each of which have kept their own genetic character and language — although the German communities declined heavily during and after World War II. In general, the inhabitants of Transylvania are a varied but handsome people. This girl represents the Romanian-speaking majority, derived from an ancient mixture of Thracian, Ostrogothic and other European components.

Fig. 81 Peasant elder from Transylvania, revealing the strong personality that marks the faces of these rural peoples. In general, the population of the lower central Transylvanian valleys are more mesocephalic, and those of the Carpathian mountains more brachycephalic — suggesting the survival of an older population in the high Transylvanian Alps.

Fig. 82 Yugoslavia is yet another complex ethnic amalgam, in which the diverse components have resisted amalgamation whether under Turkish, Austro-Hungarian or Communist government. Its archaeological history reveals it to have been, along with other Balkan countries, one of the oldest centers of Neolithic civilization in the world. Subsequent Germanic and Slavic settlement occurred, and its mountainous terrain encouraged the survival of local ethnic loyalties. These horsemen live in Sinj, a mountainous territory close to the Dalmatian coast, and are classed as Serbs.

YUGOSLAVIA

Fig. 83 The Serbs are the largest of Yugoslavia's diverse Slavic-speaking ethnic groups, and include the Serbs proper, the Bosnians, the Herzegovinians and the Dalmatians. The Southern Slavs entered the Balkans in post-Roman times, but the Balkans preserve many pre-Slavic genetic elements, ranging from early Mediterranean and Dinaric to the more Nordic Illyrian and Gothic, and to intrusive Turkic components. The Serbs are genetically the most historically Slavic of the Slavic-speaking Balkan peoples, although even they reveal the influence of the older Dinaric population.

Fig. 84 The Slovenes represent a quite distinctive Southern Slavic minority in Yugoslavia, a country whose main basis for unity seems to be a common Slavic language and a common fear of subordination to other more powerful nations and states. They are related to the Croats, but may represent a survival of older Illyrian and Celtic stock absorbed by the incoming Slavic peoples. Slovenes have been historically dominant in the former Austrian (now Yugoslavian) province of Carniola.

Fig. 85 The Croats are one of the more distinctive and nationalistic of the many Yugoslav minorities, strongly resisting Serbian dominance and anxious to create an independent breakaway state of their own. Their more northerly situation, close to Austria and Hungary, has also given them a different history, but in general they are more Dinaric than their neighbors.

Fig. 86 Another Croat female portraying extreme Dinaric influences. Compare this woman with the Macedonians in Figure 89, who represent a combination of Dinaric and Osmanli Turkic genetic influence. In general the Croats tend to be darker haired and eyed than their Slovene neighbors to the north.

YUGOSLAVIA

Fig. 87 Of the many mountainous areas, Herzegovinia is one of the more remote and distinctive. Herzegovinia is a Serbian province adjacent to Montenegro. The population is divided between Moslems and Catholics, the latter representing the original pre-Turkic Dinaric-type population, being taller and lighter-skinned than the Moslems.

Fig. 88 Montenegrins are also strongly conscious of their ethnic identity, falling as they do partially in Yugoslavia and partially in Albania. Their numbers are small, but their clanlike loyalties remain strong, and they refused to abandon their Greek Orthodox religion despite centuries of Turkish rule. Montenegrins are the tallest people in Europe, and are generally lighter in hair and eye color than their neighbors, frequently producing individuals who are golden blond. Their generally broad faces are marked by hawk-beaked noses, creating an impressive general physical appearance.

YUGOSLAVIA

Fig. 89 Of all the minorities in Yugoslavia, the Macedonians are perhaps the most distinctive physically. They bear little resemblance, and only slight genetic links, to the Macedonians of Alexander the Great's day, since Macedonia was much influenced by centuries of Ottoman rule. However, Macedonians still feel a strong sense of ethnic identity, and frequently express the wish for closer ties with Macedonians living in western Bulgaria.

Fig. 90 Albania is well known for its ancient tribal structure. Although it has been under a strong Communist central government following World War II, the Albanian communist leaders have remained nationally-minded. Famed for their fighting abilities, this Albanian is clearly from the pre-Communist period. Generally speaking, Albania may represent a survival area of the ancient Illyrians.

ALBANIA

Fig. 91 An Albanian matron from the plain of Proscipa. The so-called Dinaric strain is once again evident here. Many of the populations of the West Balkans have been described as Dinaric (after the Dinaric mountain range in Yugoslavia) referring notably to their distinctive high foreheads, prominent aquiline noses, and skulls which do not protrude backwards over the nape of the neck. Albanians preserved their tribal structure into modern times, and are closely inbreeding in their habits. In general they differ from their Montenegrin neighbors by reflecting a stronger Mediterranean component, and by slightly darker coloring of hair and eyes.

Fig. 92 Bulgaria was once inhabited by the famed Thracian mounted warriors, who were related to the Greeks, but today the country derives its present language from Slavic settlers, and its name from the Bulgars, who came from the East European steppelands, bearing a Ugrian name, but who acquired Slavic speech and a predominately European genetic character. The non-European elements sometimes to be found probably derive mainly from Ottoman Turkish influence, although most Turkish settlers withdrew from Bulgaria after World War I.

GREECE

Fig. 93 It is well known that the Greeks of today do not resemble the Greeks of the Homeric or Classical period, on the evidence from archaeological and from classical literature. While the ancient Greeks had come into Greece from the Danubian area, Greece's tragic history, since its incorporation into first the Roman then the Ottoman empires, has resulted in marked Asian influences. This Greek from Laconia nevertheless reveals a Balkan rather than an Asian appearance.

Fig. 94 From Attica we find another example of a Greek who has preserved, as have many of the village and island folk, something of the ancient Greek physiognomy. It must be realized that although the Greek-speaking peoples who gave Greece its name were essentially Nordic in appearance, having entered Greece in a succession of waves from the Danubian Valley, begining around 2000 B.C. and ending about 1000 B.C., they seemingly did not eliminate the original Mediterranean population (which was essentially similar in skeletal form and merely darker in hair, eye and skin color), but for centuries dominated these as a slave or helot class.

GREECE 111

Fig. 95 This woman may be regarded as representative of the Greek stereotype of the present century.

Fig. 96 The widespread Asian influence present in Greek cities is exemplified by this portrait of a young Greek male of the present century. The mainland cities absorbed large numbers of Asian Greeks who fled Turkey following the Greek independence struggle. When the Eastern Roman empire was overrun by the Ottomans, large numbers of Greek colonies that had been established in Asia Minor came under Moslem control. Their inhabitants did not always leave until the present century, by which time they had become ethnically quite different from their Classical Greek forebears.

Fig. 97 Crete is not totally Greek, and like many of the islands its ethnic history has been different from that of the mainland cities, especially in having evaded the population movements which affected the mainland. The main element on Crete may therefore be Minoan, with a heavy Dorian Greek overlay which is responsible for a high percentage of blondness.

Fig. 98 The "Great Russians" are the easternmost of the Russian peoples, but although they live adjacent to numerous Finno-Ugric minorities, they have in general retained the ancient Slavic type — possibly due to the sharp cultural divide that separated them from the circumpolar peoples. With their high foreheads and straight narrow noses, they would look like Scandinavian Nordics, if it were not for their somewhat heavier jaws.

Fig. 99 A blond "White Russian" girl, with the rounded face and slightly snubbed nose often found amongst the Western Slavs — presumably from absorption of Baltic peoples into the Slavic population. While it is probable that the ancient Slavs were blond, considerable Scandinavian genes entered Russia when the Vikings sailed and settled along the major rivers of Russia, and indeed the name "Russia" itself derives from Viking settlers, who were referred to as "Rus" or red-heads.

Fig. 100 A less Nordic Russian woman, working in a factory in Valogda, situated some 300 miles east of Leningrad, whose appearance indicates the influence of Finno-Ugric populations which still survive to the north and east of this province.

Fig. 101 The Ukrainians are a Slavic-speaking people whose language is closer to Russian but is not regarded as Russian. Inhabiting the rich plains to the south of Russia, the Ukrainians have endeavored to maintain their identity, despite communist emphasis on the concept of the international 'Soviet' man and woman.

Fig. 102 The name of the Cossacks is famed for boldness in warfare. Traditionally a scourge of settled communities, the Cossacks retain an ancient steppeland love of horses and warfare. Portrayed here is a Cossack from the Kuban area, just north of the Caucasus.

Fig. 103 Like many other members of persistent ethnic groups, the Cossacks inbreed closely, and this group picture shows a marked uniformity of facial features. The Cossacks may well be direct descendants of the steppeland, horse-riding Indo-Europeans of three thousand or more years ago.

Fig. 104 South of the Kuban, the Caucasus mountains (which inspired early anthropologists to give the name "Caucasian" to the "White" races of the world) are divided by steep valleys which have sheltered a wide variety of languages and gene pools. The appearance of the peoples of the Caucasus varies slightly, but in general all are European in appearance, with variations in the direction of Middle Eastern Armenoid stock.

AVAR

Fig. 105 Also once greatly feared are the Avars, another fierce horse-riding people who swept in from the steppes to attack sedentary populations. Although originally related to the Huns, they acquired a predominantly European character by interbreeding during their period of dominance, but since their defeat by the Turks they have largely inbreeding.

MODERN EUROPE

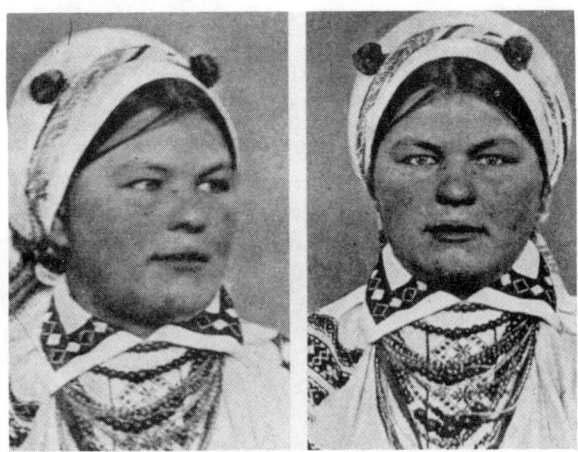

Fig. 106 This photograph of a woman from Volhynia, an area which is now largely Ukrainian, shows the penetration of Mongoloid genetic influences into central Soviet European territory.

Fig. 107 Asian influence is more clear in the case of residents of the Mari Republic, in the Volga basin, who speak a Ugrian language. The Mari Republic is bordered on the south by the Tatar Republic, although the Mari actually speak a Finnish dialect and are akin to the Mordavians with whom they are generally grouped as "Volga Finns." Also related are the Permiaks. Finno-Permiaks are a major division of the Finno-Ugrian language group, the other division being the Ugrian-Magyars, with whom the Voguls and Ostiaks are to be grouped.

Fig. 108 Other ethnic elements prominent in Europe, but akin to Asian peoples, are the Lapps of northern Scandinavia and the USSR, and the Samoyeds of the northern European USSR. Portrayed here is a Lapp woman whose appearance suggests, as with most Lapps, some infusion of European genes.

LAPPLAND 125

Fig. 109 This portrait presents a Lapp male, whose appearance differs considerably from the female shown in Fig. 108, thus further indicating that a substantial admixture of genes may have taken place in this population. The importance of the Lapps in the modern world is not their number (which is only around 30,000) but the genetic influence they are exerting and will presumably continue to exert on the Scandinavian peoples, as they are steadily absorbed into the Swedish and Norwegian populations.

Fig. 110 Finally, we present a representative of another non-European people who have for many centuries been widely distributed throughout Europe. This is a Gypsy woman from Andalusia, in southern Spain. Now identified as having originated in northwestern India, over the centuries the Gypsies seem to have absorbed genes from their host populations. Although folklore ascribes this to the theft of children by the Gypsies, it is more probably due to Gypsy acceptance of genetic input from the surrounding population by other more legal means. Thus the appearance of Gypsies varies very much from one part of Europe to another, although always something of their exotic history shows itself in their features.

MAP

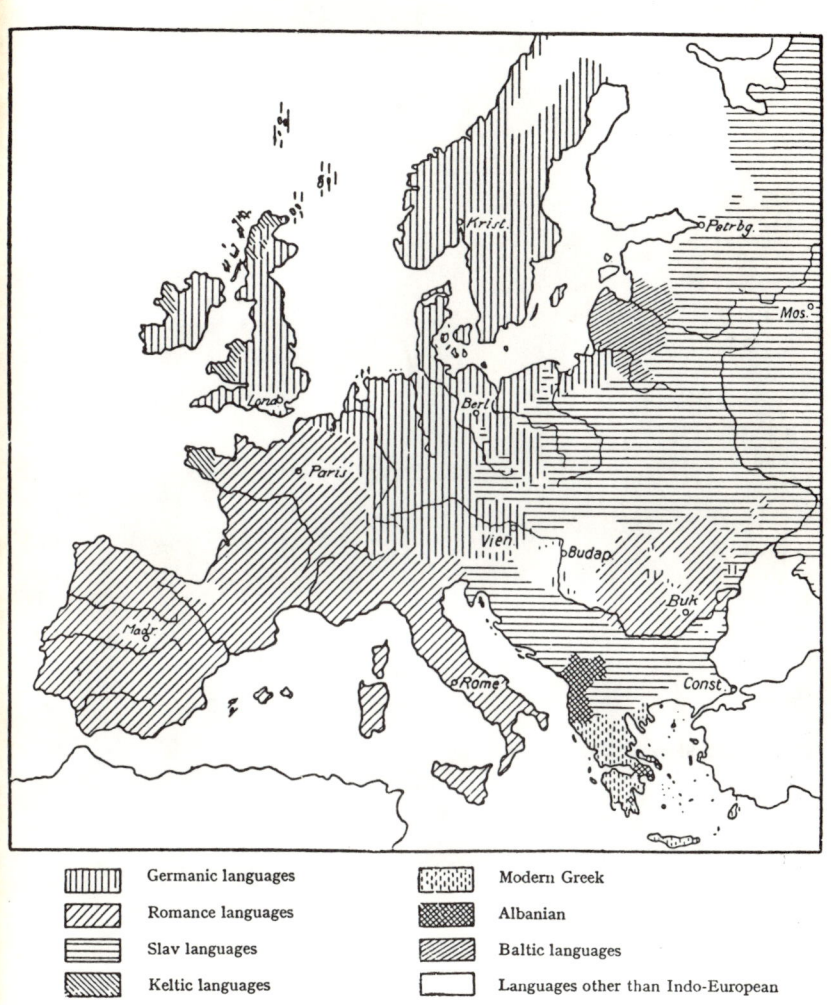

Traditional distribution of the languages of Europe (prior to 1945).

INDEX

England	17
Scotland	21
Wales	23
Ireland	24
Faeroes	28
Iceland	29
Norway	30
Sweden	34
Denmark	38
Germany	39
Austria	47
The Netherlands	48
Belgium	49
Finland	50
Estonia	52
Latvia	53
Lithuania	54
France	55
Spain	61
Portugal	65
Switzerland	67
Italy	71
Poland	83
Czechoslovakia	87
Hungary	92
Romania	94
Yugoslavia	98
Albania	106
Bulgaria	108
Greece	109
Crete	113
Russia	114
Ukraine	117
Cossack	118
Avar	121
Mari	123
Lappland	124
Gypsy	126